Never Too *Late*

Charles L. Wolfe

authorHOUSE®

AuthorHouse™ LLC
1663 Liberty Drive
Bloomington, IN 47403
www.authorhouse.com
Phone: 1-800-839-8640

Published by AuthorHouse   09/14/2013

ISBN: 978-1-4918-1070-5 (sc)
ISBN: 978-1-4918-1069-9 (e)

Library of Congress Control Number: 2013915403

Any people depicted in stock imagery provided by Thinkstock are models, and such images are being used for illustrative purposes only.
Certain stock imagery © Thinkstock.

This book is printed on acid-free paper.

Because of the dynamic nature of the Internet, any web addresses or links contained in this book may have changed since publication and may no longer be valid. The views expressed in this work are solely those of the author and do not necessarily reflect the views of the publisher, and the publisher hereby disclaims any responsibility for them.

Dedication

In appreciation of my family for their encouragement
and love. Special appreciation to my daughter-in-law
Sandy for review and suggestions.

Contents

Wedding Vow 1

Turn Back The Hands Of Time 2

To Soar Like An Eagle 4

God Made 5

A Dog Named Spot 6

I May Be My Own Grandpa 7

A Shiny Moment Of Time 8

God Shared A Blessing 9

Bread And Scrape 10

Gone But Not Forgotten 11

Vagabond 12

Butterfly Dance 14

Cloud Shadows 15

How Do I Make It ? 16

Crystal Dawn And Beauteous Night 17

Springtime 18

End Of The Brown Fedora 19

Gandy Dancer 20

Hazel Eyes 22

For Us 23

Horns Did Blare, Drums Did Roll 24

Love In A Photo 26

I Caught A Tear 28

Abiding Grace 29

I Love Love 30

A Winter's Night 32

The Old Wooden Icebox 33

A Generous Piece Of Pumpkin Pie 34

Comeupance 35

My Inside Outside Hat 36
I Smile To Myself 38
My God, My Hope 39
First Discovery 40
I'm Cookin' 41
A Boy And Four Girls 42
The King's English 43
It Must Be Done 44
Jonathan 45
Why Not Him 46
Simple Things 48
Lady At The Pier 49
Life Goes On 50
I Walk The Fields Of Heaven 51
Love Unchained 52
Mimosa 53
I Met A Man 54
The Prize 56
Misty Moments 57
Raggedy 58
Sirocco Winds 60
Hard Times, Good Times 61
My Misty Love 62
Tales We Tell 63
In My Waning Years 64
Song Of The Christmas Tree 65
Myriad 66
Lost 67
Never Too Late 68
Nov 1, 2011 70
Our Conversations 71
The Caress 72
Proud The Weeping Willow 73
The Fountain 74
Save The Gallant Warriors 76
My Friend 77
The Tire Ride 78
Shootout 80

Stage 4 82
The Untrammeled... 83
Story Tellers.. 84
To Be So Bold 85
Flowers For Naom 86
Moments Missed.. 88
Touch Of Hope... 89
Where Are We ? 90
At Evergreen... 91
Jimmy Showed Me Joy 92
Sometimes... 94
The Crest 96

Wedding Vow

Had I naught but love to give,
it would be the greatest gift by far
than all the treasures of the earth
and the wonders of the farthest star.
I relinquish now all that I am
to you my beloved, my wife, my friend.

Turn Back The Hands Of Time

Let's turn back the hands of time
to when you first said you were mine.

Let's live again those early years
when only joy could give us tears.

We'll raise again a family,
our happy children, you and me.

Let's erase all the saddened hours
and replace them with this love of ours.

God once more will fill our days,
in all His wondrous and blessed ways.

No one can know the fullness of life
which we share as man and wife.

Darling I want to live them again
until God decides to give them end.

So bow with me with tender heart,
as time grows near that we should part.

In memory those times we'll share
and leave our future in God's care.

To Soar Like An Eagle

The joy of success is so uplifting;
the joy of it, the thrill of it,
to win, to succeed,
using abilities to rise to the highest level,
how satisfying.
At the right moment one feels uplifted
as if soaring.
The sun is brighter, flowers have special aroma,
the rush as if walking on air, soaring within,
confidence heightened, and
pride is a motivator for whatever the future holds.
Oh, how the eagle must feel as it soars, with
prey in hand, toward the utmost heights, having
been successful.
To soar in spirit, as does the eagle, a goal
worth the striving.

God Made

God made me—God made you.
God made monkeys and the fishes too.
Some say not and many say true,
and some would say from fish we grew.
It's funny though that I can't swim a stroke,
so I'm sure what they're saying is just a joke.
But our God knows sure, so we know it's true,
for His word professes as His creation we grew.
My faith is solid and in Him I trust,
so I'll walk this earth as He says I must.
Think what you will and think what you may,
but I'm going to walk in God's appointed way.

A Dog Named Spot

To most eyes he was a cur, a misbegotten
left over from a brood of pups.
To me he was a prince, with spotted hair,
hazel eyes and frizzy tail.
Oh, his tongue would loll, loosely
hanging, dripping dog spittle in a puddle
as he panted and looked for a pat, his lips
seemingly presenting a sign of gratitude,
but he was my beauty, hard not to love,
and close to heel as we strolled along,
quick to find a favored lap,
head tilted at the least awareness of
my quandaries, a friend in time of
silent reverie, happy to respond.
A boyhood memory amid happy
thoughts of bygone times.

I May Be My Own Grandpa

A funny thing happened as I searched my family tree.
I found that my nearest grandpa was really me.
How did it happen? I searched and easily found
a census that showed me born in a little town
to my father who had the same name as me.
He also had his father's name, again the same as me.
It also showed the dates that were given for our birth
matched exactly, and I thought "What on earth?".
Digging even further my mother was my wife,
and my father was my son whom I had obeyed all my life.
My sister was my aunt which was a big surprise
which made me really confused about our family ties.
I would stop there but there's more to the tale.
As I searched further our relationships began to pale.
I found that we were neighbors and not of family.
I'm sorta kinda confused, as you can see handily.
I'm going to have a family talk to see what's about.
Being myself is bad enough as I have found out.
So wish me luck as I bring them all together,
to see whether I get to keep my current Dad and Mother.

A Shiny Moment Of Time

Have you seen him- the hurt, the lost,
closed into himself,
in the world but not part of it,
buried in his thoughts,
unspeaking,
unrevealing,
alone.
Have you felt him—
his hurt, his sadness, his need?
Have you reached out to him,
to make for him a shiny moment in time?
For if you have, you too have felt
that shiny moment in time.
God bless!

God Shared A Blessing

God shared a blessing one day,
filled with beauty, grace and gentleness,
to bring me joy for a time.
A treasure of love for my keeping,
to cherish it beyond measure,
to receive from it great pleasure,
to be returned only at His asking.
God shared a blessing one day
which in my heart shall last a lifetime.

Bread And Scrape

As a youngster I loved bread and scrape.
It came to me lovingly from caring hands.
How it came is a story I just have to tell
for it lingers in my thoughts with loving care.
A kind neighbor lady would care for us kids
while Mom went to work wherever she could.
I came into the house hungry asking for food
but the fare was skimpy and sadly I stood
while she found some bread and margarine too.
Quite seriously she asked did I want only the
bread or bread and scrape.
Getting excited I thrust out my hand and
pleaded "Bread and scrape! Bread and scrape!"
With wide strokes of a knife she lathered a
crust and then deftly removed the spread
leaving just enough for taste.
Often after that we played the game, and
I would leave with a pat on the head and
join her son at play.
She was the first Negro person I ever met,
and my heart and mind hold her fondly.

Gone But Not Forgotten

The pleasures we miss by quick decision,
the times we rue lost advantage,
like the word dispatched and not retrievable,
how depressing when understood.
Time is a thief capturing the moment and
stealing away, seldom returning the forgotten,
never consoling nor offering the same opportunity
which unheralded is lost.
Grieving are the souls seeking but unable to
reclaim moments lost in the rush of time,
in heart and mind worth a kings ransom.
Love lost, feelings shattered, respect lost,
all because a moment is now gone, gone, gone.
A thought, a hesitation may make the difference,
if we have the time.

Vagabond

"Roots and stones, roots and stones,"
and a yielding sigh.
Down the lane, it was a bumpy lane,
shuffled the woebegone soul,
haggard, tattered, dejected,
head bowed,
torn shoes a doorway to each pebble,
each twig; step by step;
a far cry from better times;
dark passages of memory refusing entry;
hope grasped, waning, discarded;
"Roots and stones, roots and stones."

The tree shadowed way seemed devoid
of promise.
Slowly, whispering sounds disturbing
thoughts, the shaggy head, eyes weaving side
to side, raised with uncertainty, ears
attentive to every sound.
Scurrying squirrels, bee buzzes, bird chirps,
and rustling leaves introduced awareness in
the still air.

Awakening recognition stirred long
sleeping memories of nature's works.
Tears coursed craggy cheeks as other memories,
forced into nothingness, awoke,
returning spirit, hope and promise.
Sunlight, responding to the moment,
brightened the end of the trail.
Step by step urgency prodded,
with a sobbing refrain,
"Going home. Going home."

Butterfly Dance

Colors, colors, colors,
swirling, fluttering,
wafting on the wind;
every zephyr an opportunity,
a panoramic display
in rainbow absence,
beauty defying senses;
blossom to blossom,
meadow to meadow,
pond reflections of images
magnificent against the blue sky;
Swallow Tails, Clippers,
Isabellas, Orange Tigers,
and Monarchs, majestically join
in the kaleidoscopic beauty
of the butterfly dance.
All is still, all is at peace,
the world a forgotten place.

Cloud Shadows

Cloud shadows on the field,
soft blows the wind as bearded grain
sway back and forth
from gold to tan and back again,
dancing to the flow,
preening before a glowing sun,
and God smiles.

How Do I Make It?

I wonder at times during the activities of life,
How do I make it? How do I deal with strife?

Then I remember my Lord at Calvary,
how He dealt with strife just to save me.

How He gave of himself unselfishly
and carried His doom to make us free.

How do I make it? I'll tell you how!
Christ in my heart guides me now.

Crystal Dawn And Beauteous Night

Morning. Snow blanketed trees as far as the eye can see,
a grand new world.
I look, with rapid heart beat and soaring wonder, at God's
splendor.
Oh, to stop the world and time that I might revel as sunrays
lend their glitter to the panorama before me.
Day hastens on as I strive to keep mental images
of my crystal dawn, and the cardinal highlights itself for me.

Night time, full is the moon, and still the snow lingers,
but with new glory.
Tree limbs, crested with snow, their shadows wafting
across drifting realms below, provide a dark beauty as
magnificent as my crystal dawn.
Prints in the snow herald the passage of the lone traveler, as
full moonlight, glowing through the gently waving
limbs, illuminates signs of the journey.

From crystal dawn to beauteous night wonder is my realm.
At loss are those who see not the splendor and magnificence
that purposely God has laid before all.

Springtime

Slowly, slowly rise the greens and a myriad of
hues,
as, amid softness of the day, peeps and chirps
float skyward, lofted by soft breezes.
Tenderly the doe gentles her newborn fawn
near a bubbling spring, freed from its winter
slumber.
Profusions of buds dot landscapes reaching
skyward to present crowning glories as they
escape confinement waving a sweet hello to
all nature.
Carefully the nest of the robin forms in the
crook of a budding elm soon to fill with
eager mouths seeking a mother's chosen
repast.
Springtime has arrived.

End Of The Brown Fedora

Tumble, tumble, tumble,
in the gutter, on a walk,
through sun and rain,
the old brown fedora is driven by the wind.
Who knows the life of this fedora?
Who knows its possible thoughts?
Perhaps once a regal crown of a gentleman
or shelter for a penniless vagabond;
witness to their many deeds and misdeeds,
cloaked in the history of its benefactors;
once well groomed, shaped to fit a regal head,
now bedraggled, every smudge and wrinkle
giving evidence to its many travels;
a toy for the elements,
tossed hither and yon, finally tattered
and forgotten.
Pity the fedora if you will, lonesome in
its memories of wondrous days,
the bearer of bits and pieces of the souls
to whom it catered.

Gandy Dancer

If you've never worked on a railroad, you probably don't know what a "gandy dancer" is. Well, a "gandy dancer" is a who and not a what.

I pleasured myself several summers as a young man by working as a section hand (a laborer on a railroad track repair crew). The work was hard, mainly pick and shovel stuff with a few hundred wooden ties and steel rails and tons of ballast rock provided for amusement. We dug up the old ties and rock replacing them with new and an occasional new rail when necessary. It was hot sweaty work, aggravated by the incessant prodding of the foreman. We were young. We worked hard with an appropriate grumbling rejoinder for the foreman. On occasion we would make the opportunity to hunt for wild strawberries along the right of way (the property bordering on the tracks), and for a very few moments we pleasured ourselves in the savory taste of our find. One of our largest projects was to replace rail over a nine mile long section. For that, our small crew needed help. Several bunk cars of itinerant workers were brought to the site to help with the task. Before their arrival, we were told of the forth coming arrival of these "gandy dancers". For sure, I just knew that "gandy dancer" was a belittling name, so I never used it in the presence of these men.

Years later I learned that when the Transcontinental Railroad was being built, tools used on the job were made by the G and D Tool Company. A worker, using a G and D shovel, would pry up the end of a wooden tie, which was under the rails, and bounce on it while another worker would push rock under the tie to support the rail. The person on the end of the shovel was called a "gandy (G and D) dancer".

I am so very proud to have been a "gandy dancer" in my lifetime.

Hazel Eyes

She was real to me,
just a passerby to others.
For me, no one else existed.
Her hazel eyes,
highlighted by her smile,
held my heart as we passed.
A wisp of auburn hair,
floating gently in the breeze,
framing her winsome smile,
are still real to me,
now sealed in my mind,
ever in my thoughts
with those hazel eyes
so precious to me.

For Us

Sweat stained blood upon the garden wall,
shed there by Christ for us all;
left again upon a cross, such a tragic loss.
A gain not a loss for you and me,
but a loss for God who gave so free
a precious son of treasured worth,
sent to cleanse a sinful earth
and rise from a tomb to make it true
He came to save both me and you.
He said that He would come again
and to prepare our hearts to meet Him then.
On any day as the sun rises high
expect to see Him in the sky.
It was for us he cried,
for us He died.

Horns Did Blare, Drums Did Roll

There was a hill which we did ride,
few cars to bother our downward glide,
our bicycles fit with balloon tires for speed and
handlebars with ribbons, which a good racer needs.
"No hands! No hands! or your out of the race."
No hands to steer or you'd surely lose face.

Then came a parade on the Fourth of July.
An opportunity arose that could not be denied.
In step they marched as the band loudly played.
With a gleam in our eyes, the decision was made.

Shirt tails flying and the wind in our hair,
"No hands!" rang out as we shouted the dare.
"Look out! Look out!", the spectators cried,
but we of stout heart would not be denied.

Down we sped as horns did blare,
and the beat of the drums boomed through the air.
Down we flew past all the host
of marchers and spectators crying, "Coast! Coast!"
From the corner of my eye I saw a judge glare
and a patrolman did nothing as with open mouth
he stared.
On we sped despite every shout and stare
and near the leader we stopped with a proper flair.
The horns did blare and the drums grew loud
as with satisfied hearts we bowed to the crowd.

Love In A Photo

In a frame on a bureau the photo of a couple
showed clearly their happiness,
he smiling broadly at the camera, but she,
in an adoring way, eyes sparkling, looked
tenderly upon him, smiling at his happiness.
It wasn't noticeable at first viewing, but on
a closer review, the thrill of her moment
could clutch the viewer's heart with the sense
of joy that only love could project.
The hope is that he, too, grasped the moment
and rejoiced with her while the mood was
captured for eternity.
The voice of a photo saying love, love, love.

It was the first photo of my wife Naomi and I together.
It is in a family album, and over the years I've seen it
innumerable times, glancing at it as I did at others.
Now as I view it, I see the happiness in her eyes. I never
noticed that before. It was there all the time and, now as I
look at it, the realization of her happiness thrills me beyond
measure. Why did I not see it before?

I suppose my own happiness blanketed my awareness. I was always focused on her smile. There was such a joy shown, that at a glance I failed to see the love reflected in her eyes. I guess I could feel sad when I know what I had not seen, but the sight of it now is too thrilling and satisfying for sadness. To live that moment again with greater awareness would magnify my love of her, if that is possible.

I Caught A Tear

I caught a tear.
I remember well the dearest eye
from which it fell.
I let it on my finger lie,
the first to fall when she cried.
My truest love so tender, so sweet,
I could not let it fall to her feet.
I would have it now had it not dried,
yet I hold it in me, deep inside.
If I could, I would have kept that
little drop, but in too short a time
it disappeared.
Sadly, as I saw it go, a tear of my own
followed swiftly, hurrying to unite.
How glorious a feeling of love and sadness,
still felt, still desired.

Abiding Grace

There is a promise I hold in my heart of God's abiding grace,
not some poetic phrase that leaves a fleeting trace,
but a gift of love assured to me by His sacrificial Lamb.
Because of that I grasp the promise of His eternal love,
a reminder to us all that love is always sharing
with each other and not a random call.
If we take hold of this promise and do not let it go
from heart or mind, the world can be a better place
for people of every kind.

I Love Love

Call me a romantic.
Call me a dreamer.
I love love.

I love to feel its inspiration,
its rightness.
I love the romance of love.
I love its joy and excitement,
the thrill of its power,
how it overwhelms and joins.
I love its forgiveness and
understanding.
I love how the beguiled
lovingly embrace.
I love each precious moment
of love.

I love love in nature.
I love the leafing tree as it
lifts itself lovingly to the sun,
the rose as it lovingly opens
its petals to show its beauty,
the robin lovingly feeding its
young,
and the autumn leaves lovingly
on display.

I love the stars and moon as
they lovingly present a haven
for lovers.

I love love for its permanence
and ageless truth,
beyond life, beyond death
unto the realm of Heaven.
I love having loved with wonder
the love of my life.
I love the love of God
who loves even me.

Call me a romantic.
Call me a dreamer.
I love love as surely as love has
loved me.

A Winter's Night

Shadows on the snow making
silhouettes in the bright moon glow,

as clouds beyond lend sailing ships
and mountain peaks to the night.

Trees with crested branches sway
gently in the cool breezes.

Footprints large and small wander
aimlessly down country lanes.

Silver glows the night as peace
abides.

Beauty reigns over a world at sleep,
and all is quiet

The Old Wooden Icebox

The old wooden icebox, I remember it well.
For quite a spell, our family had one.
It served us well through the summer heat.
We had ice chips as a treat from a cake of ice.
One of my chores weekly was to hurry and go
to the nearest ice plant pulling my wagon.
So, as fast as I could, I hurried away
and brought back a small cake of ice.
Up the stairs to the apartment I carried
it, wrapped in a burlap bag.
As the ice melted, it drained into a pan
under the ice box. By turns we boys would
empty it, usually out a window.
Came winter time and the cold outside
was nature's ice box.
The ledge of the window would hold some food,
and a metal milk box was used for milk delivery.
Some mornings found the cream had popped up
frozen with the bottle cap on top.
Life was a little more enjoyable with our
old wooden icebox.

A Generous Piece
Of Pumpkin Pie

I stopped in at a diner to get a bite to eat.
They didn't have a hostess and just waved me to a seat.

They didn't have a menu and just quoted what they had.
The selections that I pondered weren't any better than bad.

So, I opted for desert and coffee not too hot,
which was splashed into a mug from an old porcelain pot.

The pie I was served was pumpkin with whipping on the top,
but the fly stuck in the middle made the offering a flop.

As I ate around the creature it began to flip a wing
and struggle to lift off from the gooey, fluffy thing.

With a spoon I dug it out and threw it on the floor.
The owner grabbed me by the seat and threw me out the door.

I lost my appetite and mumbled with a sigh,
"I'll never, ever, ever eat a generous piece of pumpkin pie."

Comeupance

It's sort of an old time word,
one you've probably never heard.
If you ever have gotten in trouble,
It's a word that'll make you think double.
Whenever a trouble was of great substance,
I'd hear, "Just wait, you'll get your comeuppance."
Then into the picture would come
one who didn't like a lot of humdrum (a word
usually misused).
I would be lectured for my utter nonsense
with the warning, "You young scamp, you'll
get your comeuppance if you keep it up."
and a "Don't do it again!"
It's sort of like "You'll rue the day!"
but much stronger in every way.
You can tell me I'll get punished,
but please don't say my comeuppance,
since it admits to things of great substance.
Just say, "I'll spank your pants
for all your utter nonsense."
We have to remember, we will more
than likely get our comeuppance.
So play it "cool".

My Inside Outside Hat

I have a hat I really like.
It goes with all I wear.
The outside is blue.
The inside is gray.
I can wear it either way.
With my blue suit
I wear the outside,
but with my grey suit
I wear it inside outside.
I also have a brown suit,
and wear my hat inside outside.
Some say I should be different
and with the brown suit wear the outside
outside not the inside outside.
For me that doesn't match as well,
although being different stands out.
I like to be different at times.
So sometimes I wear my black suit
and can wear my hat inside outside or
or just outside.

The outside sheds rain better than the inside.
Depending on the weather I have a choice.
I can wear it with the outside outside
or the inside outside.
I really like my hat,
though it's getting old and worn.
My oily hair is turning the grey side inside
dark like the blue side outside.
The weather is turning the outside as light
as the grey side inside.
I'll never buy a new hat.
I'll just turn my inside outside hat
inside or outside at my whim.
I hope you're not jealous
of my inside outside hat.
Perhaps I'll let you wear it
on an inside outside day.

I Smile To Myself

Inwardly I and you live a secret life,
one we enjoy or bemoan,
one which to no one else will ever
be known.
It's a life of fancies, unfulfilled dreams,
imperfections, sorrows, moments missed,
unanswered questions, doubt, "if you knew
what I know" wisdom and a slight superiority.
At times, in the midst of surrounding events,
I have a tendency to smile to myself and
set myself apart but unmoving with a
feeling of self that I like and enjoy.
I like smiling to myself, not smugly,
but with satisfaction of my being.
No one fully knows me nor I them except
God in Heaven.
So with trust in him, trying my utmost
to let His will be in me,
I'll smile to myself and hope others can too.

My God, My Hope

This hope, my God, I have in you,
in good times and bad,
whether happy or sad.
This hope, this faith, this trust,
is my shield and my strength.
So, my Lord, I have no other course
than to trust in you.
I know not what the days may hold,
but I know your grace is sufficient
and your mercy is love.

First Discovery

"Look at me! Look at me!" a little voice squealed
as on a pudgy finger his first caterpillar crawled.
Amazement shown in wondering eyes at such
a wonderful and grand surprise.
"Ooh, look at you!" A loving mother cooed.
"Stay still now." she added.
With careful hand the child coaxed his find along.
Up it crawled so very slow to knuckle and to arm.
In wonderment and with great joy a crowd did gather
and look wistfully at the scene as it progressed
remembering each their own childhood discovery.
In time the mother explained in simple terms the value
of his find, the butterfly that would develop to bring
beauty to the world. Understanding, he gently lowered
it to a nearby bush, waved a departing kiss, skipping
happily along with joy filled eyes looking upward at his
mother and jabbering excitedly.
Those who had looked upon the scene found a new
vigor in the day because of a child's discovery,
and a butterfly flew slowly down the walk.

I'm Cookin'

I baked a cake the other day.
It fell apart, but that's okay.
Hey! I'm cookin'.

I'd never baked a cake before
and almost spilled it on the floor.
But, hey, I'm cookin'.

I peeled potatoes and boiled them good
then mashed them up like I should.
Hey! I'm cookin'.

The kitchen filled up with smoke,
and the fumes kind of made me choke.
But, who cares? I'm cookin'.

I put the fire out with foam
in order to save our little home.
But Hey! I'm still cookin'.

My hair is singed and my mustache is gone,
but in the kitchen I'll still carry on.
Hey! That's part of cookin'.

A Boy And Four Girls

A quiet walk I thought, just a reverie.
The macadam walks meandered through
lush grassed lawns, the scent of the new
mown hanging in the air.
Birds fluttered from tree to tree, and from
a pure blue sky the sun shown brightly
on the beautifully adorned park.
My reverie escaped as sounds of laughter
reached my ears, vague at first but louder as
I followed the course set before me.
Cresting a rise I beheld a gaily engaged
pubertal group racing, chasing in and out
amidst swing sets, slides and teeter totters,
a boy and four girls.
How fortunate, I thought, to be so out numbered
and overjoyed with the moment.
Oh, how my heart thrilled at the prospect as
reverie of days long past lightened my steps
away, un-interrupting a picture no artist
could truly gather.

The King's English

In years gone by the King's English was the chosen word
but now a days the way it's spoke is confusing when heard.
Without realizing what we do when in conversation,
it begs the need to return to Webster's wordy interpretation.
Often statements result in a listener's double take.
Here are a few that might make one or two heads shake.
A carpenter hit his nail when swinging at a nail.
His doctor wound a bandage around the wound.
He had an accountant who couldn't account for his account,
and his wife pinned up her slip so that it would not slip.
His son, descending the stairs, took a step on a step,
and, using his head, he became the head of a company.
His daughter said she could can- can on a large can,
but when she tried she fell on her can.
Some people have a habit of snuffing snuff
and often stuff themselves with the stuff.
Clowns huff and puff when hit in the face with a powder puff
and will try to pound a pound of dirt in a half pound can.
So simple words can mean two or more things
and we must be sure to listen,
for we never know when the definition can change
from that'n to this'n.
,

It Must Be Done

It must be done I know.
This desire, this urge, this need,
the fulfillment of God's will;
the commitment must be there
for whatever the call may be.

To be satisfied without full
assurance of total completion
can lead to shallow self-respect,
which no one in honesty desires.

If I do not have the full courage
and will, what is the total value
of my soul? Life is too short.
When God calls, it must be done.

Jonathan

God gave me Jonathan,
a hurting lad in need of solace.

Gently I rubbed his back
and sang a soft melody.

He slept.

An old man full of memories of youth
and playful, tired sons.

A return to yesterday in the
beauty of a moment.

God has ways. God has ways.

Why Not Him

"Why not me?", he thought,
      as the cry for volunteers came forth.
"Is it not the time for me to show my worth?"
"Why not me?", he queried of himself,
      as around him nervous eyes did dart.
Louder came the cry,
      persistent with anxiety shrouded.
In pondering thought he wrestled,
      his early passion clouded.
To those about he turned his eye
      and whispered, "Why not me?".
A glimmer of support issued in return
      from every eager eye.
Within his breast there grew a power
      which he could not belie,
and greater desire assailed him
      as another call rang high.
"It's more than I can do.",
      a voice said close by.
Another cried, "I'm sorry. I don't dare try."
From his throat there arose a shout,
      and his words finally rang out,
"Why not me?", as he strode to the front
      of that muted timid crowd.

Then a whisper began to grow
    into a massive scream,
"Why not him? Why not him?
    He's your man it would seem!"
From out of the crowd a powerful arm
    reached out in loving embrace,
and a voice close to his ear said,
    "I shall give sufficient grace,
so you will have the will
    to go out in my place,
to approach the world with convincing
    word and deed.
That's all I ask,
    just go and plant my seed.
My grace will be sufficient,
    and that's all that you will need."
With head up high and shoulder squared,
    he left with great desire,
to proclaim his faith to all he met
with blessed holy fire.

Simple Things

There's something about simple things,
uplifting, satisfying, reminiscent;
too often overlooked taken for granted,
dismissed.
Life is full of simple things- their innocence,
clarity, peacefulness, beauty,
calmness, unpresuming presence.
I like an ice cream cone on a whim,
a cooling breeze on a hot day,
a memory that stirs fondness,
the scent of flowers,
the multi colored rainbow,
a baby's laugh,
a playful pet,
new mown grass,
children playing without rancor,
and so much more to calm the
harshness of life and bring cheer
to weary hearts.
Oh, give me simple things as every day
pauses to stimulate awareness of good
and quench sordid realities of life.

Lady At The Pier

I saw a lady at a pier on a misty night
looking out across the rolling waves.
Heedless of my presence,
she pulled her shawl tightly around
her shivering shoulders.
Ships with their nets hanging aloft,
bobbing up and down, pulled at their moorings,
as if seeking to go again to far horizons.
Homeward trod tired seamen, glancing
occasionally over their shoulders
at an empty anchorage.
My heart panged with regret as I trudged away
knowing she would stay until the
anchorage was filled.
Fog continued to roll heavily into the harbor,
and I lost sight of her in the mist.

Life Goes On

Life goes on though you are not beside me.
Life goes on with dreams of yesterday.
I have love that you alone did give me.
It shall be my stay whatever else may be.
I have found through you my life's contentment.
My lord, my God together we will see.
Sometimes I feel great loss and sorrow,
but life goes on until we meet tomorrow.
In my heart I find neither ill nor trouble
for you are there, my anchor and my life.
No farewells or goodbyes ever given,
for we are one as life goes on.
Our lives had times of joy and pain,
whether there was loss or earthly gain.
Our hearts stayed tender despite hard times,
fulfilling our commitment and sharing of life.
Sometimes events were less than we planned,
but life went on and all became right again.
A choice is made, a corner turned,
a door may open or it may close,
and life goes on despite a right or wrong.
Hope springs anew amid the sound of weeping.
The clamor of joy introduces a new way,
and life goes on to face another day

I Walk The Fields Of Heaven

I walk the fields of heaven wherein the lilies bloom;
in my mind, in my dreams, in my prayers,
among its blossomed terraces,
arm in arm with saints of old.

I walk the streets of Heaven as I leave its blooming fields,
down to its precious garden, and therein my Saviour strolls.
With no spoken word we walk silently along.
The glowing presence of God's love lights the narrow ways.

There is no measurement of time; no year, no month, no day,
as in endlessness we go in the glory of God there,
and music, sweet and soothing, goes with us everywhere.

Love Unchained

Love,
A wisp in the span of life as a
day in the full span of time,
to be cherished, nursed,
emboldened with desire,
preserved from fading,
unsettled but not chained,
harbored in the safety of the soul.

Mimosa

Gaily Mimosa blossoms sway back and forth
as the breeze gently pushes limbs
in playful manner.
Myriad butterflies flit to and fro, some white,
some yellow, striving to catch
nectar tantalizingly awaiting them.
Honey bees in their own way hover to catch
a blossom as it passes first
one way and then another.
Majestically the Monarch rides the wave,
wings spread in wondrous pattern.
Beauty rides the air.
The humming bird, beating the air excitedly,
joins the display. Mother Nature sighs
and God smiles. All is well.
Soft clouds drift. The sun lends its radiance.

I Met A Man

I met a man;
he wasn't old, he wasn't young.
Between us a wondrous song was sung.

We spoke of this and we spoke of that,
melding as one right where we sat.
We talked of worldly things, the joy of God,
and what we faced as through life we have trod.

He has children, as do I, the apple of our eye.
How we wished for them a life
free of all the hurts of strife
in a world with nothing but peace by and by.

We spoke of all the gifts we own;
talents, abilities, God given ways
to better the times of our children's days,
and teach them well before we're gone.

We promised each other to use our gifts,
as much as we possibly could,
To better the place wherever we stood
and ease that place of strife and rifts.

Many are the times I think of that day.
Very often I bow to pray
for guidance to fulfill wherever I can
the promise I made with that special friend.

The Prize

It's not something I could have bought
and much better then what I've sought.
Full of promise, offering much,
far beyond what thoughts could touch.
I could stand on a podium and show it
while waiting joyfully for all to praise it,
but some might miss the value it offers
thinking it requires coin filled coffers.
It's a prize, free and much sought after,
full of blessings, joy and laughter.
With it comes not a cup but a scroll
soon soaked by tears of the winning soul.
The prize is not measured in terms of fame
rather in the loss of sinful shame,
giving joyous life offered with God's love,
available to all who will make it their trove.

Misty Moments

Times come when I feel the urge
to remember feelings lived;
bringing to life misty eyes, by
the first love held for a time
and released for the better;
then life love held for eternity
uninterrupted by final parting;
acceptance of God as God
with unerring trust;
memories of togetherness
and sad separation;
special happy times filled
with joy and love;
all these and other treasures
brought out from time to time
to stir heart to misty eyes,
welcomed with a smile and
wistful and refreshing recollection.

Raggedy

In my life time I've heard it said,
as if speaking of the dead,
he's a raggedy old man,
she's a raggedy old woman,
and they're a bunch of raggedy kids.
Words that cast aside the value
of the soul buried among a bundle
of shreds.
Too often first appearances are the
trade mark of misunderstanding,
when in a moment of heartless
assumption the value of a person
is mentally defined for all time.
How crude we are at times,
unknowingly relegating souls
to the realm of abnormality.

I have been a ragged little boy,
and unknowing of the world
around me, I lived in joy, for
my bundle of shreds may not
have been of value but my inner
view of simple things were my
treasure.
Now I find in better times the value
of a person is not measured by outer
appearance but by the acts of love
extended to the raggedy boy and the
raggedy soul yearning for recognition
of their worth.
So, I find raggedy is only a word
heartlessly used by a raggedy soul.

Sirocco Winds

Summer, a sea of desert beneath the feet,
a cauldron of heat;
I know not the Death Valley furnace nor
the Mojave burn,
but I do know the winds of the Sirocco,
pushing smothering blankets of fire,
wild brush shriveling under the heat
of the desert inferno,
wilting man in his search for cooling relief
in the midst of blowing sands.
The brave survive wilting passions
and sorrowful calamity,
for they know blue sky shall come
`through the hazy drift of sand,
and it is time to recover zeal, thwart
Nature's hideous garment,
win again and recover passion knowing
Sirocco winds will come but never daunt.

Hard Times, Good Times

He shuffled down the gravel road,
a little boy, his wagon in tow,
loaded with vegetables that he would
try to sell door to door.
The money would go back to home
to help the family live.
The times were hard, but all chipped in
to do whatever came to hand.
Some days were full of hunger
and some nights without heat.
They all hung together just like all
the rest, trying to do their best.
Amidst those times they could still laugh
and live in harmony.
They would hug and kiss their hurts away
although the times were bad.
When I think of their plight and that
God has supplied all my needs,
my soul does bow in reverence—
because that little boy was me.

My Misty Love

I see her in the mist from time to time.
I wave, I smile,
I cry as slowly she fades away.
Ever the vision haunts my thoughts,
my dreams;
Come back, come back, from
fading distance.
Engulf me with your presence.
My love, my love,
ever present in memory.
Ever there. Ever there.

Tales We Tell

The older we grow the larger they get,
told with bravado and no regret.
Each repeat is a tale larger than before,
flavored by superlatives once more.
The giants we've slain who can doubt.
No one was there to see the bout.
The dragons were many, our power was great.
Our tales grow each time we relate.
Growing old our dais is our history of life.
We've lived it well through good and strife.
The skeptic may raise a jaundiced eye,
but we know what we tell is not a lie,
embellished perhaps, built with flavor,
the better for the listener to savor.
They may differ each time as we forget
exactly how we told them. Yet,
they are our tales, that we've lived over time,
and we'll tell them until you sing Auld Lange Syne.
So bare with us we ask as we tell you again
the tales of our lives, and we'll be happy then.
Cronies and grandchildren will relish each tale,
and our lives will end on a grandiose scale.

In My Waning Years

Flinging wide the doors of yesterdays,
in my twilight years,
I take backward look and recover
fading memories.
Hurriedly I write them down before
my thoughts escape.
Recollection of the many and varied
moments which so quickly passed
has not always captured the full flavor
of each occurrence.
But, the thrill of part is better than the
loss of all.
Without crystal ball, I relish in the
thrill of life replayed, promises
fulfilled, successes enjoyed,
love without measure, and more good
things to come.

Song Of The Christmas Tree

Out in the forest one eve I trod with axe in hand,
seeking for a Christmas tree, the fairest in the land.
In a cove by itself stood a stately fir,
shaking, waving and bowing as the wind did stir.
On each limb I imagined balls and ribbons bright
with a string of bulbs to give color with their light,
and on the top amid garlands was brightest of all
a great star shedding its rays like a mercury shawl.
So glorious was the picture I had brought to mind,
I thought not to cut it down, and left, leaving it behind.
As I walked away, I turned to admire it once more.
Its waving limbs seemed to sigh angelic chords.
A turtle dove sang in sweet harmony.
A star above seemed to wink as I turned to go my way.
I'll never forget the moment of sweet peace I found.
It's not a tree I need for Christmas,
just a sweet angelic song.

Myriad

Thoughts, thoughts, thoughts,
questions, wonderments;
Is there? Isn't there?
Seeking, finding,
hesitancy, doubt, quandary,
accepting, rejecting.

Around and around,
back and forth;
what's next?
Troubled, troubled, troubled.

New light, new light,
God beckons.
Glorious awakening,
clarity reigns.
Peace, peace, peace.

Lost

Wide eyes staring, unseeing;
old smile replaced by slack face;
How different!
Still loved.
Perhaps listening but not hearing;
speech mute but for a faint try;
How different!
Still loved.
Dear to heart.
He was that way.
Heartbreak for we who knew
who he was-certain, loving, patient,
a brother, a friend.
Missed before his time.

Never Too Late

Growing up has been a mission,
filled with a cornucopia of events.
From childhood to youthful years:
skinned knees, tears, laughter,
hugs and kisses;
questions answered or unanswered;
feats of daring do, lessons learned;
first love, broken heart, wistfully
remembered;
nature's beauty not understood,
later reveled at with amazement and
sorrow at opportunities of wondrous
vistas lost.

New visions, growing up years:
responsibilities accepted or dismissed;
goals set, met or forgotten in the midst
of new opportunities;
childhood days revived in tales of
daring do; new adventures and temptations,
lessons learned, wisdom gained;
career time, awareness of new found talents
always there, surprisingly surfacing;

acceptance or rejection of God;
difficulties resolved or dismissed;
new love surpassing tucked away
youthful flirtations;
faithful vows setting the tone
for lifetime commitment,
new found love wrapped in coos,
don'ts and guidance; growing awareness
and responsibility; new purpose.

Graying years; wonder at their coming,
time now an enemy, too fast, too fast;
goals set, goals met;
forgiveness asked, promises kept;
old friends gone, not forgotten;
pleasant harmony sought ;
love a thing to treasure and express,
tender smiles, loving caresses a joy;
family bonding, hearts entwining;
time for atonement, time for God;
never too late, never too late.

Nov 1, 2011

Three years, five months and three days,
discovering continuing love in nature's glory.

Perhaps a smile, maybe a tear, the whisper of a kiss
or a loving touch with a sparkle in the eye;

Mimosa blooms, the humming bird, budding roses,
sources of joy from new perspectives;

Falling leaves, snow capped limbs, colors in hanging
icicles holding memories of continuing love.

God could not have planned better the metamorphose
of un-relinquished love.

Three years, five months and four days
discovering continuing love in nature's glory.

Our Conversations

Full of laughter, full of love,
I speak to you and know you hear
though you are not near.
Tears flow free as I feel your touch,
faint as the morning breeze.
Who can fathom the depths of your love
left to dwell in my heart, my mind.
Memories carry forth the times we shared
together and apart.
So, now in this waiting time,
I cherish our conversations.
I love, love you still.

The Caress

Ordinarily it may not seem to amount to much,
a pat of the hand, a stroke of the forehead,
a comforting smile, a glancing kiss - all intended
to gentle a moment, sooth anxiety, reward the
surprised, and give tender care;
but to the honoree it promises melding of hearts,
a reminder of binding love, natural, unceasingly
overwhelming, joy unbounded, life filled full.
The caress—a solution, a healer, a thrill, a sharer,
as on a drowsy afternoon a head reposing
on a lap is stroked gently by a lover's touch.
The soft velvety feel of the hand, accompanied
by a soft whisper, overflows the moment with love.
Oh, the wonder of the caress—a gift of God's grace.

Proud The Weeping Willow

How sad the weeping willow we may think at
first glance, bent to the wind, sun, and cold, rain
tears sliding to the ground, while beneath its bows
nature stirs.
Nests of birds - the warbler, fly catcher and tit -
make home in its branches and there their songs emit.
Beneath its wide spread branches low to the ground,
lovers on a picnic can often there be found.
Artists, brush in hand, find beauty amid its leaves,
as near brooks accept its languorous reflection.
How proud should be the weeping willow, though
seeming to be sad, that within its realm can be found
the soothing balm of peace and tranquility.

The Fountain

It stood off a way from the road,
a moss encrusted fountain on a dank
and gloomy day.
A lonely angel rose above its algae
watered dish.
At first I was unable to recognize
it as a fountain, perhaps once a wondrous
sight.
A lone tree, bare limbs extended, hung
limply as if struggling to guard its ward
from a pressing field of weeds.

I wondered, for a moment, at the
existence and then continued on my way.
Some time later, by chance,
I journeyed that way.
Recognizing the way, and remembering
that gloomy day, I grew curious to see
the lonely scene.
The sun shone brightly in the blue sky,
birds flitting about, happily on display.
Nearing the solitary spot, I beheld the
unexpected.

The fountain, no longer moss covered,
flowed with clear water, its basin full.
On its overflowing rim birds gathered,
displaying a multitude of colors, and
heads bowed to the basin as honoring the
angel now dressed in her finest robe.
Dripping dampness fed a surrounding field
of flowers beneath a glorious hanging willow.
Joyfully continuing on my way I felt uplifted
sure that I had seen the glory of God set into
place.

Save The Gallant Warriors

There has to be more than a world at war,
more than the grief of a child, a mother, a wife.
How tragic - warriors live and remember the gore,
never free of the horrors the rest of their lives.

There must, there must, there must be an end
to the frays
that constantly mar the breadth of man's days.
The hardy must stand up and raise protest
to be heard the world over, "Desist! Desist!"

Embraced arm in arm people must share together
a peace beyond understanding and without tether.
To share, to share the joy of free breath
is our God given right and not just a token myth.

On bended knee before our God,
remembering bloody fields men have trod.
'Beseech the Lord for a world completely free
of a need for warriors' should be our plea.

My Friend

My friend is a hard to find type of friend.
In conversation he listens silently, but
from his silence he brings answers well
thought and imparts them unassuming
and full of deep conviction.
My rhetoric is turned to the simple
and more readily understandable, in two,
three, four words. No flowery presumptions,
just a quiet statement of fact or opinion.
I find in him a sort of brotherhood, not akin to
family but of an earthy spiritual connection.
A few words with him are a boon
to a lackluster moment of time.
He need not bear me special gifts or
salutations of friendship, just the
unspoken awareness of my being.
So, I salute my friend as a friend.

The Tire Ride

On a hill two boys played
with a truck tire that had strayed.
Turn and about they tried and tried
to give that old tire a downhill ride.
Standing it upright was quite a chore.
After a failure, they tried once more.
With a tug and a pull and "Eureka! At last!",
the old tire stood steady and fast.
Into its core the bravest one did slide,
bracing himself for the grandest of rides.
"Give 'er a push.", he yelled "Give 'er a shove."
and his pal pushed and strained 'til he felt it move.
With a whoop and a holler they yelled with joy,
for they'd found themselves a real working toy.
Down the hill it rolled, the boy still inside
gritting his teeth, not letting fear still his pride.
With a "wahoo" and "whoopee" he cried his glee,
and the old tire rolled down and down past a tree.

With a bump and a bounce it came to a stop,
tipped over and ejected the boy with a 'plop'.
"My turn! My turn." Howled his oncoming friend,
"My turn and you can do it again."
To the top of the hill they rolled that old tire
and rode it again and again trying to bounce higher.
They would still be there if the day had not ended,
and took the tire home and had their wounds mended.
Who can tell what a boy can do
with an old truck tire, a stick or even a dirty old shoe.

Shootout

It was the second time Ray and I met.
He hadn't become my brother yet,
but that's for another day.
This was the time he had come to play.

What to do? What to do?
We had to think or the day was through.
A grove of trees grew near the house
and looked like a likely place to carouse.

We stood pondering and scuffing our shoes,
and as we studied an idea grew.
His eyes got big as deeply he thought,
and then he exploded, "Know what I got?!"

"See my Red Ryder. It's a fine bee-bee gun.
I think target shooting could be fun."
I hesitated to reply, uncertain and bemused,
and he looked at me with a sly grin, amused.

"Have you got a jacket we can wear?
We're about the same size, and we can share."
I heard his words, quickly understood,
and ran for my jacket as fast as I could.

Since he had the gun, he was first to shoot.
I donned the jacked and away I did scoot.
In and out I ran and the bee-bees did fly,
as I ducked my head to protect my eyes.

Turnabout we ran with yelp and whoop
as though we were part of a storming troop.
I guess the game ended even that day,
but, if I lost, that's okay. I was playing with Ray.

Just another kids' game.

Stage 4

Stage 4! Stage 4! Stage 4!
Louder, louder drum my thoughts.
Stage 4!
What is next?
Sink or cure, sink or cure,
No other chance, no other out.
Stage 4, those dreaded words.
Where is hope?
I want hope.
I want peace.
I want joy.
Oh, my dear family!
Let no one suffer.
Sink or cure.
Where is hope?
Oh, my dear God, there it is!
Hope, oh blessed hope.
Bring forth the cure.
Life must go on.
Dearly beloved we are gathered
here with hope.

The Untrammeled

A mother's true love is of undeniably honest
intent;
a love shown to a first child no more than
that shown to the second;
all intent for each the same, undivided,
encompassing all, unmeasured,
totally extended without reservation,
uniting family with conscious sharing,
each difference of the twain accepted,
caressed with care, nurtured for the special
care of each.
Her intent misjudged by the unknowledgeable
and that tenor accepted with grace for family
good. Storms of discord negated by a forgiveness
built on honest endeavor and understanding.
Mother's love, the balm, the cure, the assuager.

Story Tellers

I really like a good story teller. The one who can
get your ear and make you lean on every word.
I'm sure you've been there too. A good story teller
has all the facts straight or can make up the necessary
facts to keep a story real, real interesting.
I used to like to sit with Grandpa and listen to his
homilies of days gone by and dream I was right
there with him, hanging on every word.
I've stopped at times to listen to a group of
story tellers, each one trying to outdo the others and
creating facts unimaginable that drew me like a magnet
for the arrival of the climactic ending.
I've even tried to be a good story teller, like most everyone
has, I suppose. I'm not always too proud of the outcome,
especially when my facts don't fit for a proper eye
popping, rib tickling conclusion, and people roll their
eyes in that "this is unbelievable" expression.
But, maybe one of these days we will meet on the
right occasion and yarn away as good story tellers do,
and your eyes will pop or roll and we can enjoy a
real good conversation. Hope to see you soon.
I sure do miss my grand children's "Awe, Grandpa."
at the end of a really good whopper.

To Be So Bold

May I be so bold to confess that I
love you no less
than I did a moment ago or
will for an hour, a day, a year,
a lifetime?

May I be so bold to say,
though you seem to shy away,
my outreached hand is there
to hold?

If I had the courage,
I would be so bold,
and perhaps you would take hold
to linger for a lifetime.

To be so bold is beyond me.
So, in my weakness, I remain
not so bold and live as such
with a memory.

Flowers For Naom

When young it was my pleasure to give flowers to
young ladies. Some liked corsages and others liked nosegays.

I like nosegays with their tiny buds and wispy crepe carried
in the hand as a bride at her wedding, bringing a daintiness
and highlighting sparkling eyes.

Corsages are beautiful, not quite so dainty with their flamboyant
orchids, carnations and roses, but made to enhance the beauty of
the honoree.

And then I met Naom.

A nosegay was not practical for her, for being hand held they
had to be set aside when playing piano and organ.

Corsages for her were particularly well suited for weddings and other special occasions except for the nosegay she carried at our wedding.

Long stemmed roses and other flowers in vases were my usual gifts to her and rose buds set down in a ornate bowl of water, opening slowly and floating in their beauty. The awakening of their special beauty fascinated us, and we shared the wonder of God as though seeing our newborn.

Flowers for Naom were an awesome pleasure for me in my giddy child like joy and overwhelming love.

Moments Missed

How often opportunities come and go.
Moments of exchange missed and
longingly desired.
A hug, a kiss,
a touch offered and missed,
smothered in the haste of day.
A kind word, a supporting smile
regretfully not tendered to the sad,
the lonely, the bereaved.
Support to the work weary, the
unemployed, the homeless,
the hard of heart needful of a
sunny day, a caring friend.
Sharing of memories, happily
lived and of solace to the lost.
So uncountable and so sadly
unforgettable.
Lessons learned too late and
gifts unused.
Too late but remembered, to
prompt in other moments,
held firmly in the tender heart.

Touch Of Hope

On a little limb hung a lone leaf
over a ragged little bird with a crooked beak.
A breeze did waft and the limb did sway,
and the leaf did brush the birds feathers that day.
From a pod on the leaf some seeds did fall,
and the crooked little beak hungrily snatched them all.
Trees touched their limbs and whispered in the breeze,
and their meeting applauded the joyous scene.

Where Are We ?

Was there a time when you hurt and I
wasn't there,
or I was there but didn't show I cared
and yet did?
Was there a time when you were happy and
I was happy too,
but time and space separated us and we
didn't have a clue?
Has life become so complicated that we don't
recognize our sense of presence though we
walk together?
Is sharing so common place that it has lost
its value,
that for granted is now a way of life?
Is it time to stop, share, reflect and regroup?
Fleeting time dismisses all, but ever loving
hearts dismiss time.
The future holds the wellspring of happiness,
to be lived fully, with care, awareness and
unceasing love.
Where are we ?

At Evergreen

I have to go soon—to Evergreen.
There's someone I have to visit at Evergreen.
I often go because she means a lot to me.
I sometimes take flowers.
I try to keep her up to date on things—
things in the family—but I think she already knows.
I try to neaten the area where we are.
I think it gladdens her when I do that,
and I enjoy her presence.
On occasion I read to her after our talk,
reading poems I have written.
She's always liked my poems and listened.
Usually, when I'm done, I gently rub my hand
across our stone and wave my hand as I turn away.
I feel her smile as I leave.
Someday, when I'm extra tired, I'll rest there
for quite a time, and share with her our special place
at Evergreen.

Jimmy Showed Me Joy

Jimmy Silas lived down the road from me,
with long hair, tattered shoes and a patch on each knee.
I rode to see him often on my bicycle spanking new
and not a single envy did he show, as to his home I flew.

I often let him come with me to play with all I had, but
he'd get bored, look at the sky and say, "Boy, I'm glad!"
It puzzled me why he'd be glad and not have very much
when I had joy in all the things at home that I could touch.

His Daddy and his Mommy looked tired and all worn out
but always had a smile for me when I was playing about.
It seemed like such a mystery each time I went their way
that they had so very little and yet were carefree and gay.

Once Jimmy took me in their home and I saw all they had,
and when I saw how little it was I felt so very sad.
Jimmy saw just how I felt and taking me by the hand
led me to a corner where stood an old and well used stand.

Upon that stand there sat a book all worn from long use,
its cover tattered, its pages thin, but not from any abuse.
It appeared to have had tender care for there was within
a list of many dates and names of all his natural kin.

"This is why we're carefree and you always see us gay.
This is the Holy Bible that gives instruction for each day.
We read it every morning and kneel and bow our heads,
and on these pages you see tears of joy that we have shed.

We don't mind that we have little of any earthly thing,
as this book contains God's love that makes our heart sing.
So, as each day begins anew, we rise and go our way,
safe and secure in the truth that God will be our stay.

Would you like to pray to God and feel His presence here?
He's loving and kind. There's nothing you should fear."
In awe and some confusion I knelt with my dear friend,
and there I met with God until I did fully understand.

That was many years ago, a time I'll not forget,
nor will I look back on that time with sadness or regret.
Each morning I kneel humbly before I start my day,
my tear stained Bible in my hands as joyfully I pray.

Sometimes

Sometimes you're enjoying a breeze,
then pollen makes you sneeze,
but the breeze continues to waft,
and you sigh and slowly relax.

Sometimes we're feeling the blues,
life seems full of bad news,
and then someone slaps us on the back
and gets our mind back on track.

Sometimes I think back
imagining things life has lacked,
and then I remember
family Christmases in December.

Sometimes I wonder why
loved ones have to die,
and try to understand
why it's a part of God's plan.

Sometimes, when I'm alone
in melancholy, to which I'm prone,
somebody special comes along,
and my heart sings a song.

Sometimes the world seems upside down,
a smile turned into a frown,
then I stand on my head,
and lo, there's nothing to dread.

Sometimes life seems too perfect - sometimes.

The Crest

It was a vision for me, not to be shared.
After a several mile trek, I drove to the crest
of my hill, looking forward to Autumn leaves
bright in beauty before the sunny,cloudy sky.

I had taken this way before, in other Autumns,
each time beautiful, but different from the one before,
leaves in a multitude of colors decorating the country side,
and I had gasped and rejoiced at the beauty before me.

This drive was no different except for the one who
accompanied me, anxiously awaiting what I would share.
As we reached the crest of our hill, all splendor burst
forth beyond our expectations. Glory reigned, sunshine
beamed and our hearts responded as natural love
united our spirits in the sharing.

In that special moment, our appreciation for God's
artistic disclosure enveloped we two as one
and our return, though met with beauty, never
seemed to match our special time of reaching the crest.